Ten Sure Signs You Are Not "Dating 101"

by

Antoinette Nyiann Lawson

authorHOUSE™

1663 LIBERTY DRIVE, SUITE 200
BLOOMINGTON, INDIANA 47403
(800) 839-8640
WWW.AUTHORHOUSE.COM

First published by AuthorHouse 05/2305

ISBN: 1-4208-5772-X (sc)

Printed in the United States of America
Bloomington, Indiana

This book is printed on acid-free paper.

"Self-Research"

No relationship is perfect.
In the absence of love, hate will develop.
The answer is not then to abort love, but recreate an
environment where both man and woman can exist.
We accept death without understanding life.
Well-meaning people with good intentions seem to be the
main ones with no direction.
Decisions are not taught to meet the needs of the
consensus, rather to meet the needs of those with
negotiable co-opted concerns.
Relationships enable an ongoing basis for love and hate to
mirror one another,
yet at the same time be empowered by it.
Relationships are supposed to echo reciprocals of feelings
that are mutual between man and woman from which both
benefit.
Failing to seek different outcomes by holding onto past
shortcomings recreates the same conditions from which
one came.
To avoid replicating the same mistakes, participate in a self-
survey and see where you place your self-worth.

Acknowledgments

I think what makes my writing style unique is my
honesty. I am pulling my writings from a sincere
place, my heart. I was able to let my heart guide
me—something I'm sure everyone can relate to.
Everyone has been hurt before. Sometimes when you
are hurt, you don't know how to heal. A lot of times,
women act in haste. We do things that feel right at the
moment, and suffer the consequences as they come.

Pain is not easy to cope with. It will take you through
different stages, phases, and avenues. The hardest part
is to understand pain—peeling through each layer
of that onion until you get to the core. What I have
learned is that you can't get over anything until you
are true to yourself. It does not matter how or what
you have to do to get over him.

Understand that when you do, there's a whole other
world of chance and opportunity out there. It's a
world filled with joy and hope. You just overlooked
it because at the time, you chose to see only what
you wanted. I can share my experience of pain and

heartache because I now reap the benefits of that other world of joy and hope. I endured a lot of pain, but it only built up my stamina.

Everyone measures their joy by different measures. My joy comes from getting my self-worth back. That feeling of joy you get just from being alone, not worrying if another promise will be broken or another lie will be told. Frankly, I've heard it all before. I've learned to move to my own pace and bop to my own beat.

I remember a time when natural coordination seemed impossible. My body felt like it was going through physical therapy. I had to retrain my body of its mechanical movements. How to remove myself from that stationed position I'd been in on the sofa for hours. How to get in and out of bed, and much less the ability to remove the sheets from my body to get up to shower, eat, or relieve myself.

I had to retrain my body to get back to its regulated eating habits, and its regulated sleeping habits. I found myself so depressed, I could not muster up an appetite. I isolated myself from the world. It was just God, my thoughts, and I. I prayed and I prayed. Finally, it came to me. I finally understood that it was really over. I had to make myself understand Standard English. I had to tell myself that if this thing/situation ended, than what was it that was keeping me from starting over?

I really have to thank my sister, because once I came out of seclusion, she played a major role in my life. I can vividly recall sitting with my sister and telling her that I wanted to write a book. She then told me that I could do it. She said that God puts everyone on this Earth for a reason, and that my purpose and gift was to write. From that point, I remember calling her house hours on end for months. "Like how does this sound?" Or "What about this?"

I also cannot end without thanking my main inspiration. Without him I could have never put a paragraph together, much less a sentence. I would have never thought I would be thanking him for breaking my heart. I'm sure the tissue stocks where booming at that time. So thanks for everything, Mr. Grief. Thank you for depriving and depraving me all in one go-around. But mostly for depriving me of happiness and introducing me to the opposite of just that. Thank you for introducing me to a lifestyle where pain and sadness mirrored one another, and thanks to everyone else for being my support systems.

Last but not forgotten, a special round of extended apologies for those persons who got caught in my wrath. Hey, I never meant to extend the pain that was extended to me onto you all. I was just trying to lighten the load. Just note it was never personal. My intentions for the most part were always good. Special thanks to AuthorHouse for respecting my craft, and for believing in me and understanding that this is the start of beautiful beginnings. Stay tuned for the next book to follow, *A Woman's Intuitions*.

Introduction

We all have been introduced to life. Some of us just
were brought into life with different beliefs and value
systems. Overall, life is really not that difficult. Humans just
complicate it. We have preconditions that have been set in
place for us like laws and rules, or various other things to
give us basic fundamental structure. Yet, time after time, we
go against the grain.

We all have choices in life. Not all may be clear-cut, but
we all have choices. We all work nine-to-fives. Hence,
not all abide by the same legal codes when doing so.
Relationships are no different; either you're in a relationship
or you're not. There is no alternative to that unless you are
infringing on someone else's rights. There are just some
things in life that simply can't be dichotomized and function
accordingly.

There comes a time in everyone's life when you have to
do a self-evaluation. If you continue to trip over the same
shoe, is that the person's fault that left it there or your own
because you knew it was there and still tripped? As women,
we tend to say that "he was not the right one," but we never

say why he was not the right one. Or we never look at the part we played in the relationship.

Sometimes we get so caught up and complacent with what works, we shy away from change. Or maybe we are not even aware of what we are doing. Either way, change starts inward, then outward, not in reverse. Ladies, if you ever notice, you can change your relationship by getting into a new one. However, if you don't change yourself, you are going to get the same type of man. Granted, this one may be more educated or more attractive than the last few. Hence, they all have the same characteristics traits because you continue to seek what's not yours.

Can you remember torturing yourself wondering if he was with someone else? Did she love him the way you loved him; could she? Did he care that you cried yourself to sleep every night? Can you remember waking up every day replaying a memory of a memory? Can you remember the last words that you heard from your significant other were "Baby, I promise I will be right back?" Then you fall in love all over again, remembering what love once felt like. If so, I'd like to introduce you into a world, my world. Welcome to the world of heartache and heartbreak.

You can't imagine what it feels like to run from yourself, or can you? Have you ever found yourself in an almost situation? You know, a situation where you felt you were almost the girlfriend. Ladies, understand that there is a difference between being with someone and being with someone. It's no different from listening to someone but not hearing that person. Here is the difference: If you can't recall any talks or actions that may lead you to becoming the girlfriend, then it is not in the works. If most of the times spent between the two of you are spent in the bedroom, you are with him, but not in the way that will give you longevity.

Weigh out the pros and cons. Some guys are worth the wait. You just have to ask yourself, what are you waiting for? Are you waiting on him to finish his schooling? Are you waiting on him to get established in his career? Or are you waiting on him to leave his girlfriend or wife? The difference in what you are waiting for can help you determine how long you are willing to wait. If he feels the two of you should revisit talks of a relationship based on career/schooling, that's something worth waiting for.

Relationships are hard enough. At least once he is established in his career/schooling, that gives him more time to focus on your likes and dislikes, as opposed to him being so focused on his goals that he loses focus on trying to find your likes and dislikes. Now, if you are waiting on him to leave his girlfriend or wife, you will probably go through the rest of your life waiting. We lose patience when we have to wait in line too long for groceries, but reserve all our patience waiting on someone else's man.

The difference between waiting on a man who is trying to get established in his career/schooling versus waiting on someone to leave his girlfriend or wife is that once he gets established in his career/schooling, the plan is for him to invest more time in your relationship. When you are waiting on a man to leave his girlfriend or wife, the situation will never change. He may in fact leave his girlfriend for you, but will he then leave you for another girl?

Once you figure you are going to wait, remember, men are different from women. They will not go cold turkey. If we as women feel he is the "one," we will cut everyone off. Men pace themselves. If you don't notice a change in him, you are just there to bide time. You are no different from his favorite hobby (you are something he loves to "do"). We are taught to be optimistic and celebrate life. We are not taught to accept that things will end. We have to understand that it is okay for things to end, and as one thing ends, better things began.

Note that no matter if he is already in a relationship or not, if he does not want to commit to you; he will never be yours anyway. Ladies, word to the wise, create a checklist. As I continue to state, we have to check ourselves every so often. Here is a little sampler to get you on your way of knowing yourself better.

You Are or You Are Not Self-Checklist

___ *You know what building he lives in, but not the apartment.*
___ *You have never met his parents and he still lives at home.*
___ *You have never met nor had a discussion about meeting his parents or any other immediate family members.*

___ *You only know him by an alias.*

___ *You know his first name, but you don't know his last name.*

___ *You know he has a job, but you're just not sure what he does.*

___ *If you were ever in a bind, you could never count on him.*

___ *You don't feel comfortable bringing him around any of your girlfriends.*

___ *He has a new number, but you don't have it.*

___ *His cell phone is always off when he is with you.*

___ *He doesn't remember your birthday.*

___ *He told you he does not celebrate Valentine's Day.*

___ *He only calls you at inappropriate hours (anytime after midnight).*

___ *He only calls at times he knows you're not available (during working hours, while you're in class/seminar, or while you're at church), to avoid speaking with you for long lengths of time or at all.*

___ *He's never stuck with anything longer than six months.*

___ *You find feminine products around his house (trust me, they do not belong to his mother).*

___ *He calls you from his home, and blocks his number.*

___ *You call him from a known number and he does not pick up.*

___ *You call him from a blocked number or any number other than your own, and he picks up.*

___ *You cannot spend the night with him.*

___ *He never spends the night with you.*

___ *You have to call before you come over.*

___ *You have been with him for longer than one year, and still have no title.*

_____ *You've been with him for longer than one year, and still have no anniversary date.*

_____ *You have been with him for longer than one year and he makes someone else his main squeeze.*

_____ *He has keys to your apartment, and you have none for his.*

_____ *You've taken him out on your birthday.*

_____ *He did not ask you to attend his graduation/promotional party.*

Ladies! If you answered yes to any one of these questions above, you clearly are not the one, and you clearly need to read this whole book along with attending a self-esteem seminar.

1. Go with your gut. Sometimes we think everything has to be complex. That's why men say we think too much. Nine times out of ten, we give men too much credit. We don't want to believe they are being deceitful, so we give them alibis. How do we do this? By choosing to believe what is told to us, knowing it is not true.

Case in Point:
If he is always telling you he is hard at work. Humans do not work seven days per week. At least that was the case, last I checked. Then there are some things that just are. You know the good old lipstick on the collar, or the scent of perfume. Surely you didn't believe him when he told you that he bought it like that? Did the dog eat his homework too?

2. Know your position. Are you his friend or are you his woman? Is he your man or is he someone else's?

Case in Point:
If you don't have his home phone number, you are not his woman. If he never picks up when you call, but returns your call hours later, chances are you are not his woman. Chances are he was with another woman, perhaps his girlfriend. If he does not acknowledge your presence outside of the bedroom, you are not his woman. If you are not sure whether you are the friend or the girlfriend, you are not the girlfriend.

Ladies, if you were traveling on a boat to get to County X, would you or would you not look on that boat to ensure that it was in fact going to the destination you wanted. So why do we treat relationships any different? Is it a friendship or a relationship? Depending on which ship you are on will determine your role. If it is a friendship you seek, do not overstep your position. This is for one reason and one reason only. Unless you are able to handle what may come, never ask questions you cannot handle the answers to. Don't ask who is beeping in on the other end while he is on the phone with you. That's a girlfriend question.

Ladies, let me ask another question. If he did in fact state who was on the other end, would you continue your dealings with him? Case in point once again, ladies. Don't fault him for what you allow him to do to you. Do you have the ability to answer his telephone/cell phone if it rings? Does the opportunity ever present itself for you to answer his telephone/cell phone? Or does his telephone/cell phone move every time he does?

You can tackle this one in one of two ways. Unless you've been in any of the stated scenarios, it is not as clear-cut as it seems. Sometimes women get caught up trying to portray Ms. Joe Cool. The one who does not bring up the intense questions because they don't want to complicate things (but really they do). Again, you can either tackle the question head-on, or you can opt to not ask because you are afraid of what the outcome may be.

Don't be afraid to dive into deep "waters." You may find that it's not as deep as you thought it was. In other words, what you thought you wanted might not turn out to be what you thought it would be. But you will never find out unless you ask. Also note, if you never ask for what you want, you may never get what you want. Ladies, I just want to take the time to backtrack to ensure that we are still on the same page and I'm not getting ahead of myself.

When I stated that we are intimidated to ask complicated questions, I am not referring to questions that must be asked whether you are the girlfriend or not. You need to know his health status (last time tested for STDs, are heart attacks hereditary in his family). You need to know if he has a job or not, and what is the nature of it. You need to know if he has a wife or girlfriend. You need to know how many kids he has or if there are any on the way. If he does have children, does he take care of them (financially, mentally, and emotionally)? Now, once you gather all this information, what you do with it is solely up to you; just remember to place blame accordingly!

If you are not the girlfriend, you still have every right to ask any question you want. You can ask where he was all day. You can ask, why hasn't he returned your phone call(s) from last week? You can ask where he was on any given holiday (Thanksgiving, Christmas, New Years and Valentine's). You can ask how his family is doing. You can ask when you are going to meet his parents. But just be able to handle the response you solicit. If you are not the girlfriend, you can't get girlfriend responses.

Some women are watching football, but think they are watching basketball. If you are not his girlfriend, you have to remember there are certain boundaries. Some things just do not concern you. Don't confuse what happens at night with what happens in the morning. If this sounds harsh, don't put yourself in harm's way. Set some limits for yourself and stop compromising yourself. Doesn't the truth hurt?

Sometimes by not asking, the other person may assume you are content with how things are going. I mean, after all, you are not complaining. So why fix something that is not broken? I really could sympathize with both perspectives, but can you?

3.   If you make your bed, lie in it.

Case in Point:

If he told you that he wanted only a friend. Only a friend translates into him not spelling out that he shares his time with multiple women; read between the lines. A ladies' man will always tell you that a relationship is not something you look for, but rather something that just happens. A man tells you from the beginning that the two of you will lay all your cards on the table and see if the two of you could make a hand out of it. A ladies' man tells you tales. A ladies' man tells you he is not looking for a relationship, but yet, he is always looking for a friend, or two, or three. Why is it they can *look* for a friend, but not a relationship?

A man tells you that the best relationships derive from friendships. A ladies' man tells you that he only wants to be friends. Consequently, what do you do? You listen, but hear what you what to hear, translating what he told you into meaning that he only wants a friend now because the two of you are just getting to know one another. However, his outlook will change as time goes on, allowing the two of you to take forward steps. A man treats you the way a lady should be treated at all times and at all costs. You don't have to translate anything he tells you because he will always speak clearly and precisely.

A ladies' man tells you that he has his share of *friends* to allow him to have no set ties to any of you. In turn, you all have no set ties to him. A man tells you what's going on from the beginning. He will define every role each woman plays in his life, because he is tired of cutting corners. A man, for the most part, has realized where he messed up in the past. He has dealt with his shortcomings and has redefined himself into a one-woman man.

If you are sleeping with someone and you have no title, chances are he just wants a cuddle buddy, a homie lover friend, a secret Santa, someone to warm the other side of the bed for him. Or whatever choice words he is using to describe your situation. But remember, whatever he is calling it; he is not calling it a relationship. And for the love of GOD, please do not fall in love. If you do, blame yourself. Lastly, spare your girlfriends the late-night phone calls; they have their own problems. Besides, you're only going to get their man on the other end telling you that she is asleep and he will tell her that you called.

Okay. I sense some of you are staring at this book right now with a blank stare, trying to figure out if you have a ladies' man or a one-woman man. Do any of these things sound familiar or do any of these situations strike a chord?

__ *Do lines like it's not you, it's me sound familiar?*
__ *Do lines like this is going to hurt me more than it's going to hurt you sound familiar?*

4

__ Do lines like *I will only stagnate your growth* sound familiar?

__ Do lines like *we both know I'm not what you need* sound familiar?

__ Do lines like *I would rather see you leave than to stay and be hurt* sound familiar?

__ Do lines like *if it was meant to be, it would come back to you* sound familiar?

__ Do lines like *if it were up to me, we would still be together* (hence, he was the one that broke things off) sound familiar?

__ Do lines like *it's not you, it's the distance between us* sound familiar?

__ Do lines like *I am not where you are at right now* sound familiar?

__ Do lines like *I just want to be friends right now* sound familiar?

__ Do lines like *I am not good enough for you* sound familiar?

__ Do lines like *my plate is full right now* sound familiar?

__ Do lines like *I need space to clear my head* sound familiar?

__ Do lines like *I am just staying with her until I can get/afford my own place* sound familiar?

__ Do lines like *I am just staying with her for the sake of our child/children* sound familiar?

__ Do lines like *I am going to divorce her, but now is just not the right time* sound familiar?

__ Do lines like *that was my sister that picked up my phone* sound familiar?

__ *Do lines like you must have dialed the wrong number sound familiar?*

__ *Do lines like that was my friend's girlfriend that you saw me with sound familiar?*

__ *Do lines like it's not what it looks like/it's not what you think sound familiar?*

__ *Do lines like I was holding her number for my friend sound familiar?*

__ *Do lines like she was drunk and she fell on me and that's how her lipstick got on my collar sound familiar?*

__ *Do lines like we were both drunk and one thing sort of led to another sound familiar?*

__ *Do lines like I only gave her my number to make you jealous sound familiar?*

__ *Do lines like I only called her once sound familiar?*

__ *Do lines like I only slept with her once, but she meant nothing to me, you are the one I love sound familiar?*

__ *Do lines like if all those other women meant something to me, then why am I here with you sound familiar?*

__ *Do lines like she is lying, you can call her right now sound familiar?*

__ *Do lines like that wasn't me sound familiar?*

__ *Do lines like I don't know what you are talking about sound familiar?*

__ *Do lines like my phone was broken, that's why I didn't know you called me sound familiar?*

__ *Do lines like I was out of town (bad frequency) when you called me sound familiar?*

__ *Do lines like it's only business that ties us (him and the other woman) together sound familiar?*

__ *Do lines like maybe your friends want me for themselves sound familiar?*

__ *Do lines like they don't want to see you happy sound familiar?*

__ *Do lines like they're jealous of our relationship sound familiar?*

__ *Do lines like she only called to see how my mother was doing sound familiar? I understand that every relationship does not end like War of the Roses, but why would she call him instead of his mother?*

Ladies! It hurts me more telling you this than it does you hearing it (yeah, I borrowed that one too from one of my exes) but you have a ladies' man. My advice to you for this one, cut that zero and get with that hero who keeps offering to do all that handy work around your house. Hello...he is not putting in all that work, time, and energy for no reason.

4. Exercise your common sense. If you are the type to fall in love instantaneously, don't play the game!

Case in Point:
As soon as the two of you met, he told you he was not looking for a stable relationship because he is career driven. There is a difference between not looking for a relationship and not looking for a relationship right now. Not looking means nowhere in the near future. Not looking right now means somewhere in the near future. Or, it could also be a nice way of saying that you are not girlfriend material. Ladies, let's be real honest with one another for a moment. Every woman is not girlfriend material and vice versa.

You can't sleep with a man on the first night and expect a relationship. Just as well as you can't have any prior dealings with any of his friends or relatives. How can he introduce you to his family, if you have already been introduced by one of his family members? I think we can all agree that it's improper etiquette for you to be reintroduced by another family member. A man never wants to be with a woman who whenever she comes around, she needs no introduction because everyone has already met her a time or two. But hey, stranger things have been known to happen.

Not looking right now could also honestly mean his career/schooling comes first, and everything else is secondary. If by chance you are still there after everything is said and done, then things could be taken from there. You have to respect a man for that. Just make sure you heard the difference in not looking and not looking right now. Hopefully, you are just as driven as he is. With that being the situation, the two of you have potential to grow together. Hence, if only one of you is driven, it never had a leg to stand on and would not have worked anyway.

More exactly, this would make not right now a nice way of saying that you are not girlfriend material. Aside from you being an around-the-way girl that everyone knows; a man does not want a woman with no goals who lacks ambition. What you should be looking for in a man is someone who personifies some of your goals. If we backtrack and you are a woman who lacks in this area, your problems are bigger than man issues, or just maybe this is one of those instances where opposites attract?

Hence, all this could be prevented if the two of you just state what you want and don't want from the beginning. There is no way you can ever get me to believe that a man or woman does not know what they want from the start. Surely, both may not be on the same page at the same time, but at some point, you both should be seeking to get there. It's at this point blame falls on your shoulders. From what my sources tell me, many women tend to get more involved once the sexual peak is past. How you start is usually how you end. You have to set the tone from the beginning. If it's a relationship you want, let it be known, as he will let it be known what he wants.

None of us are children, so we all know you are not going to dive into any relationship the first time the two of you meet. But if you get to know him and he gets to know you, and he still decides to keep things the way they are, he does not want anything more than what he is getting from you. With women, more is usually all. Since you are trying to have him see you as girlfriend material, you put your all into him, leaving nothing left for the imagination. So I have to say this, if you can get the milk for free, why buy the cow?

5. You are what you eat. If you say he is no good, and you continue to sleep with him, what does that say about your character? Don't get caught up in the blame game. Blaming him for your broken heart because you assumed he would eventually come around. "Man up!" Place blame accordingly.

Case in Point:

You continue to get into one bad relationship after the next. If you continue to date the same type of guys, how can you in turn expect different results? How are you holding your head high in the sky calling yourself a woman, yet you call him less of a man and you continue to sleep with him? Women kill me with that one. We are quick to judge other men and women as it suits us. You will trash his name to your lady friends, and praise him the next day (that is, when the two of you are on "good" terms).

We give men credit for things that should be a given. If he calls and apologizes, he gets cool points. Hello! If he did something wrong, he was supposed to apologize. Now the other side of that coin is, should you have forgiven him? Anybody can say sorry. Somebody will mean it. If you know he is the type to use sorry loosely, and you continue to forgive the unforgiven, then I guess it's okay because two sorry people equals misery (you know misery needs company).

If you are silly enough to stick around and deal with someone who is only willing to give you the bare minimum level of respect, you need to re-evaluate how you value yourself. How is it that we will get into a relationship/ situation, and don't benefit from it, yet stay in it? The difference between a bad relationship and a bad situation is first, in a bad relationship; you are the girlfriend, woman, main squeeze. In a situation, you are the home girl, the other woman, the one getting squeezed.

Now that we have separated the two, anything unhealthy you don't need. Rather, you are the girlfriend or the friend. Let me tell you how to detect whether or not you are benefiting from a relationship/situation:

___ *If he is with you only by chance, perhaps his girlfriend has his car. Perhaps he is using you to do their errands. Perhaps he was locked out of his house/car. Or he just had nothing else to do. Hence, the moment he receives a phone call, your visit is short-lived.*

___ *If you believe his pillow talk is a form of communication between the two of you.*

___ *If you find yourself doing things for him that you would not do for yourself.*

___ *If you find yourself doing things for him that he would not do for you.*

___ *If you find yourself doing things for him that you should be doing in an exclusive relationship.*

___ *If you find yourself calling him to find out why he didn't come over/call as planned.*

___ *If you find yourself calling your lady friends to ensure that you are not dimwitted for taking him back.*

___ *If you find yourself justifying yourself to your lady friends about why you are taking him back.*

___ *If you have to convince yourself that you are not doing the wrong thing for taking him back.*

___ If he is driving a car you are paying the note for.

___ If he has been staying at your apartment for so long that he has squatter's rights.

___ If you can't call his house because you know he lives with his girlfriend or wife.

___ If his number changed because of you.

___ If you find yourself crying more than laughing.

___ If you second question everything he tells you.

___ If you know his license plate number like you know your social security number.

___ If you find yourself driving past his house to confirm his whereabouts.

___ If you find yourself driving past his house just because…

Ladies! If you answered yes to just one of these questions, you clearly are not benefiting from your relationship/situation. If you answered yes to more than one of these questions, keep reading until it marinates in your subconscious.

Ladies! I have to spell this one out because some of you are just not getting this. If he is not your man, again, whether it is because he already has a girl or a wife or because you are just not the one, whatever the case may be; if you are giving out free spit shines, oral sex, head, slopping knobs and he is not your man, at this point, he never will be.

If you are letting him enter and exit your body every way possible, you are not benefiting and you never will. Stop doing things a girlfriend would do. Maybe if you gave him something to look forward to, your light would not be so dim. (I guess that is why you cannot see your errors.) Please don't believe the hype about men wanting a lady in the streets but a freak in the bed. In the back of their minds, they are saying, "Damn! If she does all this with me, than what else does she do with the next man she is with?"

As far as judging other women, we are too quick to do it. We will go back to the man, yet sever all ties to our girlfriend. Never realizing if he did it once, he'll do it twice. Especially since you clearly don't have a problem with him seeing your friends. At least, that's the message you're sending. If he does decide to perform the same act again, (regardless if it's with the same girlfriend or not) are you going to cut him off or all your girlfriends? We judge the women who sleep with the men, but never the men who sleep with the women.

It's a weird situation because here you have your friend you went to Head Start with; nevertheless you choose some man that you just met during your college years. Somehow or other, you felt you had to cut your friend loose because she had more loyalties to you than he did. How do you forgive him and not her if it takes two people to make a thing go right or wrong? You can't interchange good and bad. You either forgive both of them or you don't forgive both of them. Is there ever a case where the two ladies work on saving their relationship and 86 the bad guy?

Additionally, women make exceptions to the rules when it is in their own back yard. If you or your friend somehow manages to involve yourself with someone else's man, you don't pass judgment because it's you or your friend, the situation is then different. Don't wait until your friend does it to you to pass judgment. Don't think for one minute because she is your friend, she will not do it to you. Chances are she already did it or she is just weighing out her options.

After all, that's your friend. She probably knows your work schedule and his. She probably knows what he likes and does not like (because you ran your big mouth). Don't let what your friends do become wrong because they did it to you. Let it be wrong because they did it to another woman. Did we forget why we had a Women's Rights Movement? Stop letting men conquer and divide our unit.

If we continue to link up with men, knowing their objective is sex, then turn around and give them what they set out for, the conquering part becomes easy and the division aspect becomes child's play. Some of you ladies reading this are young (under twenty-five), but I still hold you at fault because I am sure someone told you about dealing with older men and what they wanted from you. So for all of you, I say take heed to what your elders tell you. As for those twenty-five years of age and up, I say to you GROW UP!

How many times are you going to say, "been there, and done that?" How many mistakes have to turn into lessons? Trust me, there are many lessons well learned before dying, but when is enough going to be enough? Same applies to the men. When is enough, enough? I don't want to be out in social settings seeing older brothers (I am defining older as mid- to late thirties and going) still on the brawl. At this stage of the game, I should not see older brothers out in the public eye with fitted hats and baggy jeans (throw on a button-up and some slacks). I don't want you guys rolling up on me trying to get my number by attempting to keep current with the latest street terms.

I don't want you asking me if I want to dance so you can show me the moves your teenage child showed you. You know, like the "Harlem Shake" or "The Chicken Head." At this point in the game, I expect to be asked if I would like to "Step in the Name of Love." Simply put, we all love hip-hop. However, when there is no more hop in your hip, just let it go. Trust me, the beat goes on. You will not lose your luster. If you really sit and think, you have more to lose gambling. By now, you should have a wife and kids. You should not have a Girl Friday watching your kids (might I add, the two of you did not conceive them together) while you are out trying to recap your yesteryears.

Some men truly believe they are missing something. Hey, like I tell my fourteen-year-old brother, whatever you left in the streets yesterday will be in the streets tomorrow. Why do some men continue to look for that right woman when what they are looking for is usually what's right in front of them? The right one and the perfect one are two different notions. To start, there is no perfect man or woman. Therefore, there will never be such a thing as a perfect relationship.

Where many people fall short in their relationships is when they try to change their partners or impose their ideologies onto them.

Sometimes you have to learn how to meet people where they are, and not where you expect them to be. Every person brings his or her own share of flaws into a relationship, just as you bring your share into the relationship. (If you are the type to blame the other person every time something goes wrong, then you need to re-evaluate the situation, because from where I am viewing it, it's you.)

No two people are the same. Of course the two of you will have clashes. You'll have clashes in personalities, options, over money, spirituality/religion...The reality of it all is this: As you take the time and grow together, you will learn how to deal with him, and the same goes with him learning how to deal with you. Either that or one of you is going to grow old and alone. Some men think they can continue to rock the boat. Some even went as far as tipping it over. There's just so much a woman can and will take.

I guess you all didn't hear Lenny Williams, Usher Raymond, and R. Kelly (just to name a few) when they told you how they cried, or how bad they had it, or what happens when a woman's fed up. There's just so long a woman will put up with your wheeling and dealing. You may think you have that lady in the palm of your hands because she has dealt with your inappropriate conduct for so many years. Hence, she will leave just when you least expect it. Don't think because your behaviors have been excused, they've been justified.

No matter how many years she stuck by you; no matter how many excuses she has heard and accepted from you; no matter how many times you ran some bull crap line to her that you both knew was a lie; no matter how many times she accepted your apologies; no matter how many boxes of tissues she went through crying over you; no matter how many different women's numbers she found; no matter how many women she has confronted you about; no matter how many women she has confronted because of you, you will pay for all that you put her through and then some. Everybody pays for the wrongdoings they have done sooner or later; one-way or the other; everyone pays.

6.   Honor your soul. Be true to yourself.

Case in Point:

If he can't give you what you are looking for, leave. Don't sell yourself short and accept any old man. It's okay to be alone in the sense of independence and not dependence on a man. Some women have never been without a man. They jump from one relationship into the next relationship until it gets to the point they're unaware what ship they're one. If we as women do not take the time to get in touch with ourselves, how then can we begin to tell the next man who comes along what it is we like or don't like?

Also, don't stick around with the hopes that you will somehow change him. Chances are, he will beat you at your own game. He will change you before you change him. Don't blow smoke up your own hole. If you find yourself doing things you would call or others would call out of your character, you've changed. If he is telling you that he is waiting for "Mrs. Right," then that definitely has to make you "Mrs. Right Now." Ladies, I am still not sure what part of the equation you all are missing. If you all keep adding up two plus two and you all are not getting four, what more do you need?

At what point do we sacrifice our hearts for peace of mind? Just because you love someone does not mean they have to love you back. Just because you love someone does not mean the ends are justifiable. Remember, you loving him does not mean he is obligated to love you back. Don't romanticize over what could be. Don't make future plans by yourself. Sometimes we get so caught up with the idea of what could be, we forget how things are. If you let go of the could-be's and old memories, it makes the letting go part a lot easier.

Some of us have reason to reminisce. Some women were once at that point where the two of them may have very well discussed future plans. Hence, once that moment has passed, it is no longer in the present tense. Let the old memories go so you can make new and better plans with someone who really cares about your livelihood. Don't miss what's in front of you because you continue to look behind you.

Isn't it funny when you recap on your past relationship/situation, you let one good memory overshadow ten bad memories. You don't recall all the times he said he would see you later and later never came. You don't remember calling his phone to see what was keeping him, only to be intercepted by his voicemail. You don't recall how hurt you felt, do you? You don't recall him going into the bathroom with his cell phone to then turn on running water. However, the water was not turned on to allow him to wash his hands, but to muffle the sound of his voice.

You don't recall him leaving your bed, and wondering if it was another woman's bed he would sleep in. You don't recall wanting to ask but feeling like it wasn't your place. Or, if you did ask, would you be rendering a response you could handle? After all, you were the other woman. We could say that the truth lies in your gut. That can't be true, because you lied to yourself the moment you slept with him, telling yourself you could change him. You don't recall sleeping with him that evening and seeing him out on the town that night with someone other then yourself.

You don't remember what that felt like. All these things you don't recall, but you remember that one time out of the x amount of months/years the two of you have been "together" and he made you feel like you were the only thing that mattered to him. It's better to shed more tears over laughter and joy than pain and misery. Trust me, I know!

7. Know yourself. Understand your self-worth.

Case in Point:
If every time you get out of a relationship, you find yourself changing your appearance (losing/gaining weight, cutting/growing your hair), chances are, you have self-esteem issues. If you understand your self-worth, you can understand the different relationships you enter and exit. Most importantly, if you know what you want, chances are you also know what you don't want. What would make you ever want less than the best for yourself? Who gets up and says to herself, "I'm looking for a man who will disrespect me every chance he gets?" As women, we say it's hard to leave, but what makes it easy to stay?

8. Time. Never let time keep you bonded to any relationship/situation. Don't fall into a comfort zone, staying someplace because you've made allowances

for your situation. Don't let intimidation or fear of surveying something/someone new keep you from moving forward. When you account for anything retrospectively, you never want to feel like you have wasted your time.

Case in Point:

If you've been with this person for so long that time begins to justify his actions (when you start making excuses for his excuses. He does not answer your call but you tell yourself, "I'm sure he is caught up at work."). If he is already in a relationship, your time has already been wasted. Don't be so insecure within yourself that you hold yourself back from being with someone who does not have any prior commitments. When you are with someone who's already with someone else, you only spend half of your time with him or her. Overall, they only see a half side of you. I believe, in my personal opinion, that women involve themselves with these types of men because they are not secure enough within themselves.

To experience a relationship with a man that is single is to possibly experience a relationship of your own. Which means your true self is revealed, your whole self. I wonder if that's what keeps some women withdrawn from dealing with different types of men? You get so use to being misused, you can't determine right from wrong. You began to think your suppose to be mistreated and when a man comes along to treat you with respect, you attack his character. You are either going to miss out on a good man because you are so situated with being mistreated. Or you will allow your insecurities to hold you back from experiencing an excusive and mutual relationship.

When we play the "dating game" everyone knows it's a cardinal rule that you can't tell the other how you truly feel because you make yourself vulnerable. Unless you are secure within yourself, you will keep suppressing your feelings/insecurities and the "games" continue.

9.   Know whom to call. Don't call your no-good friend, the one whose self-esteem is probably just as low as yours, if not lower.

Case in Point:

That friend is only going to tell you what you want to hear, rather than what you need to hear. That's like moving someone with a broken neck. They will only make matters worse. If you don't believe me, go to your chiropractor and tell him or her you have an STD. If neither of the two of you have a pot to piss in, or a window to through it out of, what sound advice can she honestly give you? Unless you are looking for a voice of reason (your hype person), the person who only tells you what you want to hear other than what you should hear. Or perhaps, just like you, she too is misguided and knows no better?

Don't be the type of woman who knows what she is doing is wrong, yet looks for confirmation from anywhere. Clearly you won't call your girls who are already in a relationship. For one, you don't want to sound like a home wrecker. Secondly, she will never co-sign what you are doing. So you narrow it down and whom are you left with? You are left with your no good friend who you will be arguing with next week for sleeping with the guy you told her about last week.

Here goes the irony. This is my favorite. You argue with your girlfriend for sleeping with the same guy as you. Yet you won't fault yourself for sleeping with someone else's guy. That still may not be enough for you because you still have two more no good friends just like her. You never learn until it hits home. Don't wait until it's too late. Don't think five or ten years from now when you decide to reform yourself that you are in the clear. I told you once before and I will tell you once more. Everyone pays for what they have done one way or the other. I hope you don't find one of your reformed no-good best friends with your husband. Word to the wise, quit while you are ahead.

10. Lastly but certainly not least: Leave the past in the past.

Case in Point:

Try to avoid past relationships. Maybe it's time to advance and leave obsolete relationships in their proper place. You would not renovate a new building with old supplies, would you? Embrace a new year with a new attitude. Show the world the new you, and while you are showing your new self off to the world, don't forget to take the time to look at yourself. You just might like it.

Don't make yourself a revolving door! You can't go from being the girlfriend to being the bedroom buddy. That's being demoted from a supervisory position to a regular employee. We usually want to advance towards upward mobility not downward. If you re-enter a relationship, why did you leave in the first place? For whatever it was worth, at least you had girlfriend or "wifey" status. Now you couldn't even get him to bring you a cup of soup if you had influenza.

Perhaps your motives were different. Maybe your intention was to leave with the hopes and expectations that he would change in time, and become the "man" you always hoped he would be. Which leads to my next question: If you re-enter a relationship, are you doing it with the hopes of time being the prerequisite for change and new beginnings ? If so, than where do you start? What signals you when to express your feelings for him again? What makes this time different from the last? In the process, you find yourself trying so hard to show him this "new" side of you; this "new" person you have become (partly for yourself and partly for him). Yet you have old, suppressed feelings.

Since it would be too big of a gamble telling him how you feel because you want to keep the ball in your court, you opt yet again to go with the flow. However, every time you hear the mention of his name, emotions began to overflow. You lionize over a partnership you so dearly want to forge. But, if he knew, would he respect you the same? Would the game respect you?

A part of you wants to tell him because you realize life is too short. So you imagine telling him and being rejected. Since x amount of years has not been anywhere near enough time for you to get over him, you reserve the right and the thought for another time. Taking the gamble this time a longer run will exist for the two of you, you weigh out your options, and play your part until a window of opportunity arises.

This time only, you'll remember your past weaknesses and make them your future strengths. Again, if loving him was your weakness before and you love him now, how then can you turn that into strength? You are faced with uncontrollable odds. Could he love you? Would he love you? Then if he did love you, would he be willing to love you and only you? Or would you be willing to except that kind of love? If you do, would you then acknowledge the fact that loving yourself and him could not exist? In turn meaning he does you more harm than good, and that anything you could love more than yourself you don't need.

You ask yourself again, what did you learn after that heartfelt x amount of years? Then you remember what you promised yourself. If the two paths should **ever** cross again, it would be called by your shots or none would be called at all. Now you reach the day where you are forced to cross such a path yet again. Will you fall short or stand tall? Until you can honestly answer that one burning question in the pit of your heart and soul, you decide to stay away. If you come back to that question and you realize you can handle things on your terms, only at that point do you decide if he is worth the risk or not. But if you go back to that same burning question and realize that you can't handle it, you walk away forever wondering **what if**?

However, I don't want to leave anyone with a sense of total hopelessness. Despite the fact that every one of us may have that burning love for only one person in this lifetime, unfortunate or not, that is the nature of the game. You loving someone and that someone not loving you, or not knowing how to love you the way you need them to love you. For me, I realized that I would love him until love no longer exists. No matter if either of us is married to others. No matter if he passes this life and I remain. The only things I can do for my self-preservation is acknowledge it, be true to myself, and learn how to live with coping tactics.

I understand now that you can't stop yourself from loving someone; it either happens with time, or time continues to happen. If you are like me, and time continues to happen, you have to time your time and use your time wisely. With that, I learned how to focus on coping with love that can't be given to the one I want and wait for GOD to show me who I should give my love to. Keep the faith. Keep GOD first, and everything else shall follow. If you don't do anything else, pray. Confide in your GOD, whatever your GOD may be.

"Am I a Woman/Am I Woman Enough"

With you, bad news was good news.
I too learned why "Lady Day Sang the Blues."
Arrested eyes used to cry out from something they did not do.
All because they didn't know what else to do.
I tried to keep my eye on you and the sparrow.
I suppose my reach was too narrow.
I never realized loving myself and you could not co-exist.
We exchanged sex on several occasions.
Ironically, sexual occasions became special occasions.
He'd miss occasions like birthdays and graduations; but
somehow or other always made it
on time for sexual occasions.
Mama taught me at an early age how to count my ones,
twos and threes.
I never thought I would be using those very numbers to
remind myself just how many times he'd deceive me.
Mama also told me, "Never talk to strangers."
Had I listened, I would not have had so many empty
hangers in my closet.
I want to know what makes women stay.

At what point do we no longer do for men what we would not do for ourselves?

What keeps their eyes wide and bright, while ours remain closed and dim?

Is it in the eye of the beholder or something found, as we get older?

I want to know, as women, why do we try to salvage leftovers?

What is left to talk about, if it's all already spelled out?

Why do we turn undeniable actions into maybe?

Why do we tell ourselves it's our fault things soured?

Why does everything in our body scream HIM, HIM, HIM, HIM, HIM!

They say maybe if we realized lies for lies, and up from down, we won't have to follow.

They also say misery is in the company you keep.

Since we are the keepers of our company, joy and pain, why then do we continue to invite

pain in with a welcome mat and opened arms?

We as women tend to live the life of chameleons. We change with every man we get.

Excuse me, we allow them to change us.

For quite some time, I blamed men for the increasing pain that grew within me.

Finally, I asked myself, "Am I a woman, am I woman enough?"

I can't tell you what makes a man a man. However, I can tell you what makes a woman a woman.

A woman is one who never compromises herself, her worth, or her beliefs under any circumstances.

A woman is one who takes ownership for her mistakes.

A woman understands that a man can only do to her what she allows him to do to her.

A woman understands that it is more to her womanhood than her vertical and horizontal positions.
A woman understands that a man and a woman make a unit.
A woman understands that a boy and a woman destroy that very unit.
A woman knows the difference between a man and a boy.
A woman knows her womanhood is not measured by her numerical years on this Earth.
A woman knows what it means to say she is a woman.
A woman never has to be questioned about her womanhood
A woman never has to question or second-guess her womanhood.
A woman never has to ask, "Am I a woman, am I woman enough?"

Outro

Dear ladies,

By the time this book reaches you, I hope it reaches you in the best of health. Hopefully by the time you all get this, I too will have found the meaning of what it is to be a woman. My situation was no different from what many of you may have gone through or are still going through. I fell in love with a man who fell in love with someone else. However, it wasn't all bad. The bad just outweighed the good. Hence, none of that mattered to me because I was in love. Because I loved him, I tried to stretch my love for both of us. As basic common sense would have it, anything you stretch too much eventually pops.

Sometimes you tell yourself so many lies; you can't hear what he is really trying to tell you. If he told me he was busy, I accepted it. Never mind if I wanted to spend quality time, just so long as I was available for him when he needed me. I did all this for a man who could not extend common courtesy to me. I was the sidekick without realizing it. You can easily determine your position when your friends are not off limits. I overlooked the fact that he tried to talk to my friend who knew me better than I knew myself. When I confronted him, he told me that we would have never worked out anyway.

I would second-guess myself before I would question him. I started pointing out flaws within myself, never finding any in him because he was "perfect," it had to be me, I figured. I allowed him to take away everything that defined me as being a woman, as being me. While I did everything in my power to make him want me as I did him, I could not figure for the life of me why I could not make him love me. You cannot fathom this until you are at the peak of your womanhood.

My point is, just take a moment one day and reflect. Reflect on how much of yourself you gave/give, and what you did/do not get back. I even went to the length of revamping myself. I tried to be one of those cool and collected types of ladies. One who was carefree, not complaining when he did not call. Not making any mention of the outdated dates he missed. I thought guys liked women like that. I thought he liked women like that.

It was not until recently that I said to myself, if I can't be myself around someone I love, whom can I be myself with? Since, I was too afraid of the outcome if I gave him an ultimatum, I went with the flow and tried to ride the waves. I gave him chance after chance to change until it got to the point where I just gave. I sincerely believe that if you show a man love and compassion, you will get that back in return.

You just have to remember to never compromise who you are.

Ladies, it's okay to be by yourself. If you didn't realize it, you're alone right now if you are with someone who's with someone. You are alone right now if you are with someone who does not want to be with you. Here's the secret. It's okay to be alone. Get to know and love yourself again. Stop running away from yourself. The person you should be running from, you are continually running to.

This is a question that I want to leave you with that only you can answer: What is it about yourself that you can't bear to be with yourself? Ladies, some of you are not going to like what I am about to say, but I have to say it anyway. Maybe whatever it is that you don't like about yourself, he doesn't like it either? If you can't stand to be by yourself, how then can you in turn expect someone else to? You have to be able to identify with yourself first, before you can identify with anyone else. Remember, change starts inward not outward. You can't change your surroundings without changing your situation as well.

Don't let this be a read where you feel worse than when you read it. I just wanted to point out what should be obvious. We see things, but they aren't always clear to us. Here are some last-minute quick pointers. I don't want to be the person who tells you all the things that you have done wrong yet leave you without a way to right your wrongs. Remember when the teacher used to give you your test back with big red x's to mark all your errors? However, it was very rare that you received your test back with the corrections as well. Hence, the next time you see the question, you get it wrong again because no one gave you the right answer.

Ladies, you will have your day. Sooner or later, he will get sloppy. At some point, he will test the waters. He will become so comfortable that in his mind, there are no wrongs he could commit. Thus far, you have made all his wrongs right. You have knowingly taken him back when everything pointed to his doings being wrong. Remember, it was you who never questioned his whereabouts.

You were the one who allowed him to enter and exit your body without justifiable causes. You were the one who did things only a girlfriend should do. You were the one who stuck around because you thought you would change him. Now because of all the things that you have done, he feels he is untouchable. He feels he is able to place his cup on the table without a coaster. He thinks he is so debonair and charismatic that he will eventually play himself out.

Anything done too much becomes unwanted. He'll continue with his bad habits. He'll continue to drop by as he pleases and call at will. He'll continue to use his discretion when choosing to decide whether or not he wants to pick up when you call him. At some point, all this begins to replay in your head until enough is enough. Sadly, he won't realize it until he is as stinking as a man on a toilet bowl without toilet paper.

Men don't realize women go through different phases. They don't realize their lack of calling and affection giving is what gives women time to regroup and regain composure. In the beginning, there's not much he has to do to be forgiven. In the middle, a simple call may do or any explanation to explain his shady behaviors. The end phase is just that. Nothing can help him.

In the beginning, we'll take any explanation. Even the ones we know are bald-faced lies. Now we enter the middle phase. Like I said, this is the middle phase, so generally, everything here is a 50/50 shot. However, at the final phase, there is nothing he could ever say or do to make her want him again. Nevertheless, by not really grasping the magnitude of the situation, he will try everything she wanted him to do in the beginning and middle phase.

He'll take note of her tone and change in body language. He hears the change in her choice words. Taking note of all this, he recalls the things she said in the beginning and middle phases. He'll start calling more. He is now offering to do more for her (taking her different places, taking notice of her interests, complimenting her on any changes she has made). He'll even go as far as owning up to his indecencies. What he does not realize is that it's just too late.

Every woman's closure process is different. Sometimes you are not stable or strong enough to tell him what you really want to say without him breaking down your barricades. If you are one who has to express your feelings in order to get closer, mail him a letter. If you are one of the unfortunate women who never found out his dwellings, write a letter to yourself. You can keep it as a re-read (a self-reminder); or you can read it once and trash it. If you find yourself at the point were you no longer desire to call him, yet the minute he calls you, your desires resurface, change your number(s).

If you truly want to get over him, you have to stop appearing at social events he is sure to attend. I am aware that this is very hard, however, it must be done to preserve your livelihood. Sure, we all want to put on our Sunday best and show him what he's missed. On the other hand, this plan can backfire if you are not truly over him. (This is why I continue to say games are not healthy because someone has to win and someone has to lose. Personally, I'm a sore loser.)

You open the door for so many unwelcome possibilities at this point. You take the risk of seeing him with another woman. Now your mind goes elsewhere. Now you want to know why he is with someone else so soon. How long has he been with her? Careful here. Some of these questions may turn into more than thoughts. When your feelings are emotionally tied up, things tend to happen that may not have happened had you thought before you reacted. Another thing to keep in mind, if you were never his girlfriend prior to the two of you ending things, please don't ask him any questions.

What if he has little to no interest in you anymore? How would this affect you? Or perhaps he recognizes the new and improved you and wants another go-around? Will you give him another chance? I guess that lies on your initial intentions. Are you trying to get over him for yourself or for him? Meaning, are you getting over him just enough for him to "change" or are you getting over him because enough is enough?

Once enough is enough and we decide to finally end things, it's really over. Again, every woman will handle this process differently too. Some may change their phone numbers. Others may ignore your calls until you eventually get the point. Some may not be so diplomatic about it. Some may take you for the ride of your life with barely enough gas to make it to the nearest gas station. Fellas, be very careful when dealing with a woman's heart.

It's funny how courtships have changed over the generations. At what point did sex become a prerequisite for a simple movie date? Ladies! There should never be a time where you have to sell yourself short. You do not have to give out sexual favors like a buy one get one free coupon. And another thing, the moment you should ever again hear a man tell you he is single but has other women friends, RUN!

These ladies are obviously all his friends by his call. I don't know what makes you think you won't follow suit and fall in place like the rest. A man will always tell you what he wants and does not want. All you have to do is take the time and listen and stop hearing what it is you want to hear. If your five senses are still intact (sight, hearing, smell, touch, and taste), it's time you put them to use.

You **smell** smoke, that's your first sign. You **see** a fire, and you proceed to leave. You **hear** fire and you leave. You **touch** the doorknob (it's hot), and you leave. You **taste** him and you stay.

Moving forward, none of us is getting any younger. Men have to learn how to treat women like women. Women have to conduct themselves as ladies at all times. In doing so, he will have no other choice but to come to you as a gentleman would a lady.

In closing, I want to ensure I've put forward as many remedies as I could to lessen the path to heartache. I found the best way to avoid heartbreak is to experience it. Love is just as natural as death. We have to realize it will happen to all of us eventually. Once your heart has been broken, you get a better perspective on life and the reality of it all. Additionally, no one person is unsusceptible to it.

Ironically, it puts a sense of purpose and foundation in your life. That pain you experience is something that you do not want to endure again unnecessarily or bring forth to another human being. This then brings about the ability for you to grow and realize what "true" love is and what it means to experience "true" love as an adult.

Ladies, two and two still equals four. Basic math does not have to turn into calculus; it's only as hard as we make it. We have to stop working against each other and start working with one another. The strength is in the numbers. It's a new year; we have to start somewhere. Special shout out to all the women trying to struggle with everyday stressors and having broken hearts tacked onto it. And congratulations to all the strong women who finally got it all mapped out and reclaimed their womanhood. These are the women who will mold young ladies into grown women. Keep the torches burning, ladies.

I know it seems as if I came down hard on the ladies. I just wanted you all to understand your worth and value it. Clearly, it takes two to make a relationship begin as well as end. I really have to send this piece out to all men who are not aiding to the process of growth. If you are dealing with a woman, **please** have the common courtesy to treat her as such. Don't take her love and kindness for your personal gains.

If she is woman enough to tell you that she loves you, be man enough to tell her if the feelings are not mutual. If you do love her, yet you can't give her your all, let her go. Help her help herself. If you can't see her for her full potential and all the love that she wants to extend to you, allow her to leave so she can hurt and heal. By you using that woman for your selfish gains, it's only slowing her process down.

I told you before that she would leave. Consequently, once she leaves, once she reaches her final phase, all bets are off. Let's all try to come together collectively as men and women and start talking about marriages and raising families, rather than continuing to break that unit apart. If we can't do it for ourselves, let's at least do it for the generation that looks upon us for guidance.

Ladies! Now after reading all the different scenarios of inappropriate relationships/situations we allow men to take us through, do you still view yourself the same as you did before you read this book? Here is the last self-evaluation:

___ *If you still can't be alone/you still need someone else's man?*

___ *If you still think it's okay to sleep with someone and their last name is unknown to you?*

___ *If you still think someday you will change him?*

___ *If you still think you are going to meet his parents/ any other immediate family members?*

___ *If you still have no title and you have been with him for over one year?*

___ *If he still blocks his house number when he calls you?*

___ *If you still think his leaving his girlfriend or wife is in the makings? If he does leave his girlfriend or wife, do you think it would be because of you or other issues? Did you ever stop to think that he is with you because she left him? Perhaps she left him because she found out about the two of you? In such a case, would he be likely to love you or resent you? Either case, once things end with him and his girlfriend or wife, what makes you think he wants to get into something serious again? So you are screwed all the way around. When it was just the girlfriend or wife, you thought to yourself that it was okay because you only had to share him with "just" one other woman. Now you have to share him with how many? One last note regarding this matter: If he cheated on his girlfriend or wife with you, what securities did you ever have that it was or would be "just" you aside from his girlfriend or wife?*

Ladies, if you still answer yes to any one of these questions, re-read this book. If you answer yes to two or more of these questions, re-read this book and take the time to get allied with yourself. You definitely need to be by yourself for at least six months. I'm defining alone as not getting or exchanging numbers with anyone. Not meeting new "friends."

Get to know yourself. Take long walks and/or baths. Take a vacation. You may need to ask your lady friends to sit this one out for a while. Remember, this go-around is about you finding out what works and what does not work for you. You don't need your thoughts further clouded with other folks' opinions and thoughts. Once you feel you reached your peak, at that point you can then resurface and "exchange" thoughts and ideas with whomever.

Thank you all for taking the time to read and purchase my first self-published book. Here is a sneak preview of what's next to come. This book is different in the sense that I gave a face to some of the scenarios I spoke about in Ten Sure Signs You Are Not "Dating 101." This next book is about three women, which share one thing in common, men and bad decision-making. What also gives this book its uniqueness is the setting of the book. The main focus of this book is how they all share there day to day activities with one another via telephone. Note the language used in this book is intended for mature readers only.

A Woman's Intuitions

1.   The Beginning

There will always be three phrases a woman will go through throughout her life. You can look at it as the beginning, the middle, and the end; or her past, present, and future.

Her beginning is finding herself throughout life's many trials it has in store for her. This is the point where ignorance is bliss. Upon her stumbling across her many adversities, it is here she gets a better awareness of self, self-improvement, and self-empowerment. She now understands the mechanics of life and the rules of the game.

The middle point of her life is where she learns the operation of supply and demand. She has to <u>supply</u> herself with the knowledge of her past experiences so she can <u>demand</u> better results in her new experiences (whatever they may be—relationships, etc.).

Her final moves will transition her toward the end, which is really not the "end," because learning is infinite. Women go through life with certain uncertainties. Upon their uncertainties turning into certainties, they are challenged.

If a woman is aggressive and confident, both men and women will fear her. Men fear her because she can't be easily pushed over. Women fear her because she challenges their insecurities, resulting them to feel resentment and jealousy toward her. In the end, she is labeled everything but what her mama named her. In short, their insecurities will either force her into being insecure to "fit in" or becoming overly aggressive forcing her to create this image of "Mrs. Independence."

Get Over It

Splash. Great, late for work, no sleep last night, and now this... New York dirty rain puddles on my cream Armani suit.

Taxi! Take me to the nearest mental institution. *Excuse me, Miss?* Nothing! Nothing at all I just had a stressful night. Just take me to Valley Tech High School (damn man, no more good-looking guys for me).

"Good morning, Ms. Richardson!"

"Okay, you all are greeting me before I even set a good foot in the door. Let me guess, none of you did last night's assignment for Black History Month?"

"Ms. Richardson, are you okay?"

"Yes. Thanks for asking. Birthdays just have a way of getting the best of me sometimes. It has a way of reminding one how many trials in life they have been through."

"Ms. Richardson, I thought you were only twenty-five years old. I thought at that age, you were at your prime."

"Terry! What has gotten into you today?"

"Ms. Richardson, I'm sorry. It's just what I overheard my mother saying to one of her friends."

"Okay, Terry I know everything. Since you know so much, why don't you tell your classmates that you all have an essay due by Friday. Class, you all can thank 'know it all Terry' for your assignment."

"Thank you, Terry!"

"Class, this will be a two-part topic: First, I want you to think about why races were created. Next, I want you to think of any historical African American who has made a contribution to America. No two people are allowed to have the same person. Having said that, class is now dismissed."

Antoinette Nyiann Lawson

I hope someone gets me a watch for my birthday because mine seems to be broken. According to my watch, it is 4:15 P.M. and Malik is not here. Maybe he left me a message at home saying that he had some last-minute assignments to correct. Okay, my mailbox is full.

"Hey, sweet pea, this is your mom and dad calling to say happy twenty-fifth birthday and we love you."

"Lay, its La'shaun. Hit me on the hip when you get this message."

"Hey, it's E. Call either myself or La'shaun when you get in. We made reservations, so be ready no later than 8:00 P.M."

Now what if I had made plans already? I need a pair of shoes to go with that cream and camel strapless leather dress for tonight. Well, at least I finally get to wear it. I guess Malik will just come over later.

"Hey, lady, come on already!"

"Sir, you scared me half to death. Do you know how long I was down here waiting on this parking spot?"

"Do you know how long I was down here waiting on this parking spot?"

"Take it easy, buddy, it's my birthday."

"Yeah lady, and I am going into labor. Hurry up and park already, you're holding me up!"

Ah, home sweet home. This has got to be the best part of my evening thus far. Let's see, my boyfriend is MIA. Some man with a severe case of road rage just cursed me out; and now, I get to come home and unwind, and slip into my big fluffy robe and slippers.

Ring...Ring... "Hello, Ms. Richardson."

"Essence! I called you four times yesterday; where were you?"

"Who's to say? Where were you yesterday, mentally? I got your message; however, I could not make out one word except Terrell and Stephanie. Did you and Terrell break up—I mean stop dealing with one another— you know how clear you have to be with the status of relationships when it comes to black men?"

"Yeah, we stopped messing around but you would not believe why? Terrell and...and... and...Stephanie are dealing."

"What do you mean dealing, Ms. Richardson?"

"Damn it! Stop calling me Ms. Richardson! I left work an hour ago."

41

"Sorry Malaya, but what do you mean Terrell and Stephanie..."

"She is messing with him."

"Wait. I am not following you because I didn't think Terrell was real. I thought he was another one of your imaginary friends like Tupac and Hakim. I meant to say, how could she and Terrell be dealing and none of us ever met him?"

"Well you know how she and I had not spoken in a while because I was working two jobs and she had been going through her own personal issues."

"Right."

"Well, anyway, I ran into her at the mall yesterday."

"Right."

"So you know afterwards we went to lunch and started catching up. Out of nowhere she asked if I still was dealing with Terrell. It came out of nowhere because you know Stephanie is like the only sister we all know that does not revolve her topics around men. Usually we are talking about how to improve the relations with Africans and African Americans across the Diaspora."

"Right."

"Stop saying right and just listen!" So naturally, when she asked me about Terrell, my alert system came on and I said to myself, Self, she done saw him talking to some big- butt woman in the after-hours spot. Hence, never thinking she would be the big-butt woman. Then I quickly said that he was fine and abruptly changed the subject. I started asking her about her family, and how her little daughter was; also if she and Melvin patched things up. She boldly ignored my questions and asked me again how Terrell and I were doing. Before I could answer, she asked if he had a scar on his face that he had gotten when he was younger when he refused to give his jacket up to three guys after coming from a club one late night. She went on to say that if so, we are dealing with the same Terrell and had been for the past month or so.

"I said a month or so and you are just now asking me?" Then I went on to say what was the point of ever asking me, because in order to ask a question, there had to be a thought already formulated; and since it did not stop you then, what could I say to stop it now? My first honest reaction was to slap the taste out of her mouth; but being the civil-minded strong afro-centric woman I am, I simply said I hope you make it through the rest of your meal without choking on it. I left my tip and bounced.

"No sooner as I left her, my cell phone rang. It was Terrell telling me we needed to talk."

"Do you think she told him?"

"Of course she did. Anyhow, he asked if we could meet up for dinner later on. So I flew home to find something cute to wear, but for some reason, nothing was feeling cute. All I could do is replay her words and think how hurt I was. I thought I found someone special, something special, that could have blossomed into something more. I was so mad at myself for allowing my feelings to get so intense when he never once told me they were mutual. I found it hard to face him that evening because I could not be mad at him when the fault fell on me."

"Malaya, how can you say the fault was on you?"

"For one, he was not my man. He never said he wanted to be anything other than my friend. That's the problem with women sometimes. We assume too damn much. I assumed he would eventually want more because we spent so much time together. The hardest thing I ever had to do that night in all my twenty-four years was to tell myself the truth."

"Once I got to the restaurant, I went straight to the ladies' room to make sure my Halle Berry hairdo was still fine, (you know the style she had in *Swordfish*), and my Toni Braxton face was still intact. I also made sure my navy blue Fubu jean dress was hugging all the right places."

"HA! HA! HA!"

"What?"

"Girl, you know damn well you do not look like Toni Braxton. First off, you're four to six shades lighter and..."

"Anyway. When I went to be seated, Terrell looked like he had been there for a good ten minutes prior to my arrival. I didn't feel undressed with what I had on because you know I always tell you his idea of dressing up is a brand new sleeveless white undershirt, and another crisp white Hanes T-shirt over the existing one, with some baggy over dyed blue Eynce jeans, and construction Timbos. Followed by a fitted Yankees hat to match. I know my thug love. I knew that's what you were going to say, so I said it for you."

"No I was not. I now see how your assumptions got you into this predicament. Malaya, you know I was never one to judge anyone based on appearance. Our smartest scholars are thugged out."

"Once the waiter sat me down, I apologized for my tardiness. He just laughed as if it were my first time doing so. Oh! But how quick one stops laughing when one's card gets pulled. My only question to him was why didn't he tell me?" He said that he was unaware of the fact that she was my friend until I came up in a discussion they were having last night. Then he said that I should not act like we were in a committed relationship. We had no ties to one another and I was free to see whomever I wanted. More so, it was not his fault I choose not to take advantage of that fact. He proceeded to say that the only thing I could be mad at, if anything, was the fact that she was my friend; but not really because he just found out himself.

" I asked him would he still continue to she her? Girl...you would never guess what he told me."

"What?"

"He said that the situation depended on me. If I was still going to deal with him, no, but if not, that made everything fair game. I wanted to put my stiletto so far up his rectal area that he would have needed a suppository to remove it."

"Well, what did you say or do? I mean if you could have found the right response?"

"I asked him who the hell did he think he was? Then I asked him who did he think I was? I told him that I was a twenty-four-year-old black woman with no kids, highly motivated, sophisticated, intelligent, educated, very attractive, and not to mention my work credentials."

"Damn, girl. All you left out was the numbers to your last employers. Sounded more like a job interview to me. I'm teasing. Really, please go on."

"After I said what I had to say, I got up and left. I heard him saying something about he did not want to burn any bridges and that he still wanted to be friends."

"Sorry."

"Don't be, Essence. I'm not. Hurt yes, but sorry I'm not. This was an eye opener for me. A man can only do to a woman what she allows him to do to her. Take me, for example. You think if I had told him from the beginning that I wanted more than a friendship, I would be in this situation? The answer is no. For the simple fact, he would not have agreed to those terms and I could have said okay, nice knowing you. I should have stuck to my principles and not have altered them to meet his."

"Girl, no more cute guys for me."

"Yeah right."

"You'll see. From here on out, it's twos and down for me."

"What are you talking about, twos and down?"

"If you were filling out a survey, it would be based on a scale of 1-10. If 1 is classified as being the worst possible rating and 10 being classified the best possible rating. Therefore, I want only the unattractive men. Who else wants them? This way we can cut out all middle persons because he and I will both be on the same page. He'll know and I'll know that no one else wants him and I won't have to worry about my friends or anyone else for that matter coming down with a case of the 'what if' thoughts about him. No one will wonder what if he was my man, would he do all those things for me?"

"Malaya!"

"What?"

"You left out one critical element."

"What might that be?"

"Keeping your big mouth closed. Whether he is cute or ugly, if you continue spouting off at the mouth about how good he does the mattress 'Mambo,' everyone is going to try to get a test drive. Do you know how hard it is to find a partner that knows how to do the mattress 'Mambo'? Why do you think it took me so long to leave what's his name?"

"True that." They share laughs. "Anyway, let me get ready."

"Oh, Malay!"

"Did you tell La'shaun?"

"Hell no! She is off the hook. She'll be ready to fight and calling him and her everything but God's children."

"You are stupid. Just be ready by eight."

The Middle

Someone once told me that it takes a fool
to learn that love doesn't love. Someone
else also told me that it takes a trained fool
to learn that someone does not love him
or her yet continue to love that someone
who does not love them unconditionally.
Consequently, no one has ever told me what
to do to get out of a bad situation.

No one has ever told me that there was a
difference between love and lust, and that
I should not trust someone because they
"said" they loved me. No one told me trust
is something earned and love is something
you give with the hopes that it would not
be taken for granted (with the hopes that it
would be returned).

Since I was never told, I am telling you.
Separate truth from fiction. Don't let his
street diction dictate where he puts his

stick in your body. Your body is for the one who walks you down the aisle. Don't give him permission to rearrange your canal and make it mainstream. No matter how persuasive his bedroom eyes may be.

Learn to embrace your womanhood and not your childhood. There is just some things in life a woman should not go through, and false heartbreak is one of them. Remember, love yourself first, and allow everything else to come to the rear.

1.800 Dial a Friend

"*Telling me this and telling me that...*" Yeah, I really need to practice what I preach, Barry. Here I am telling my girl about her man and I'll take any man. Used, old, borrowed, but never sold. Maybe it is just a generational thing. I know when my folks were growing up; it was more then just the exchange of sex between men and women. It was love and maybe sex. Now it's sex and I really like you, sort of. Speaking of sex let me call my "Mr. Fix It."

Ring...ring. "Blaktel operator, Nancy speaking, how may I direct your call?"

"Tell him Essence said what's good for the night and holla back."

"Okay Miss, your message is, 'Essence said what is good for tonight and to holler back.' "

"That will suffice."

"Thank you for using Blaktel and your message has been sent."

Ring...ring...ring...ring. "Hell...Hello."

"La'shaun!"

"What?"

"Get up! Why aren't you at work?"

"BECAUSE TODAY IS MY DAY OFF!"

"Why are you yelling? What are you doing tonight?"

"It's only Malaya's birthday and Club Jerkins is suppose to be on tonight, but go back to sleep, sorry I bothered you."

"I almost overslept. Now what's this about Club Jerkins? Is that the spot in Manhattan on Broadway where all the basketball players and rappers frequent?"

"What time do you want to roll? We can head there after Malaya's birthday dinner."

"You know how we do, the later the better."

"No, La'shaun, I know how we used to do. Stop acting like Lamont doesn't have that tail on lockdown."

"Like I said, the later the better. However, you are going to have to see if it's cool with Malaya, because you know she tries to warm the club up."

"Yeah, she does like to get there before midnight."

"No, she likes to get there before inflation. You can't squeeze a quarter out of her. Why doesn't she just say she does not want to pay?"

"I'm all for saving a dollar myself."

"Not like Malaya. That's just like that time we went to her house and she had all those candles burning, talking about she was meditating. Meditating my rear, she was trying to save money on her electric bill."

"La'shaun, you are a mess."

"You know it's true. Are we definitely going to the club tonight so I'll know how to dress?"

"Yeah, but don't get all star struck like you usually do. Most of them only want one thing—trust me, I know—being an insider an all."

"I hate when you do that."

"What? Give you advice that you are not going to take heed to anyway?"

"We all know you are the CEO of *Black Out* magazine and you brush elbows with the celebrities. That does not make you an authoritative figure on their motives."

"Just get ready and don't mention anything to Malaya. The only thing she knows is that we made reservations for her somewhere and to be ready by eight. She thinks everyone else forgot her birthday."

"I have to call her. I slept most of the day away."

"When you call, make sure she is getting ready. You know she is slower than a sloth."

A House Is Not a Home

"Going out again, hum?"

"Baby, let's not go through this again."

"So don't go out again, and again and..."

"All right, Lamont! I don't understand why we have to go through this every time I get ready to go somewhere."

"It's not just somewhere, La'shaun. I don't understand why you need to go club hopping every weekend, and you have a man?"

"That's exactly why you shouldn't be insecure."

"Don't try to run game on me with that insecure crap like I'm some lame dude you used to deal with. I'll tell you this much, your friends are not going to be the only two single for long."

"What are you saying, Lamont?"

"I'm saying you all are some MBW's."

"What?"

"Mad black women. You and your friends are always complaining about how there are no good black men and you have one right here. La'shaun, I don't know what you think you are going to find in those clubs, but you better hope whatever it is you find, you can give it back."

"Now you are accusing me of hidden indecencies?"

"Hey, if it looks like a duck, walks like a duck, quacks like a duck, chances are, it is a duck."

"Or slut you mean, right?"

"Hey, I didn't say it, you did."

"Yeah well, don't wait up for me tonight. I might take your advice and go take a swim in the nearest pond."

Girl Talk

La'shaun: "E could make a bedspring sing a song of mercy."

Malaya: Essence is nobody's slut.

La'shaun: "Pupa makes no mistakes."

Essence: Malaya, do not sweat that. Why would I let anything she says trouble me when the closest she is getting to a man is sleeping on her Tommy Hilfiger sheets.

La'shaun: At least I know his first and last name.

Essence: Oh, because you know someone's first and last name, you know that person? I mean, how well do any of us really know the men we sleep with? How long were you with Lamont again, La'shaun?

La'shaun: Long enough to know his last name, and him to know mine.

Essence: You are 100 percent right, by him knowing your last name gave him more access to get an order of protection against you. That way, you can't wait for him in front of his apartment anymore.

La'shaun: I would call you something other than what your mother named you.

Essence: As long as I am not called anything that begins with an "s." By any chance, does the word *stalker* sound familiar?

Malaya: Every time we three-way, the two of you go through this and the purpose for me calling is null and void, because by the time I get around to asking what I wanted to, one of you makes me mad and I hang up, or one of you gets mad at each other and hang up.

Essence: You are absolutely right. The floor is yours.

Malaya: I was calling so I could get some tips. I was wondering if either of you have ever had phone sex before? I am trying to step my game up a notch.

La'shaun: I did.

Essence: Anything to do with sex, you'll know I've done it.

Malaya: Did it ever feel weird?

La'shaun: The first time did because with anything new or unfamiliar, you don't know what to do. In my case, I didn't know what to say.

Malaya: Did you ever feel like the topic was forced on you?

Essence: Are you trying to tell us that he forcibly penetrated you verbally?

Malaya: That's why I don't like to mention certain things to you because you think everything is a joke.

Essence: That's not true.

La'shaun: Yeah, Essence. I would have to agree with Malaya on that one.

Essence: Simply put, I only tried to say that you need to loosen up. You have to go into certain situations with an unwary mind.

Malaya: There are just some things I am not willing to compromise. There has to be a boundary. Why is it the woman who always has to compromise?

Essence: Why does everything have to turn into the battle of the sexes with you?

Malaya: We have compromised ourselves far too long for men.

Essence: And if this were a forum for the history of the Women's Rights Movement, I probably would have given you an A+. Since this is not, I want to bring to your attention a thing called another woman. She lurks everywhere too. She is the one doing everything you won't do. She is the one you need to give your woman's rights speech to. Lovemaking is no different from your typical nine-to-five. You can get promoted or demoted all the same. Why do you work overtime?

Malaya: To show my boss that when its time for promotion, I would be the suited candidate.

La'shaun: Well you better get to working in that bedroom, girl.

Essence: Save me the "We are the World" speech. You also work overtime because you know just as well as I do that if you are not going above and beyond your normal expectations, someone else will, and you will be replaced.

Malaya: I don't know, Essence.

Essence: You just need to loosen up and stop being afraid to get your knees a little dirty.

Malaya: But what if I do it wrong?

Essence: Of course you are going to do it wrong the first time. Practice makes perfect. Just remember not to scrape, and keep your lips in formation. Plus, if you are dealing with a stand-up type of dude, he will guide you. It's not like he will tell you to stop.

La'shaun: If you are that nervous, get some tapes. Also, you can get some toys to practice on.

Essence: Personally, I would recommend a pickle. The pickle is similar in shape and size and it gives you the juice effect too.

La'shaun: Everything goes to the gutter with you, Essence. Malaya initially called about getting over the hump for phone sex, not a tutorial in oral sex 101.

Essence: As you all say, with me it's all the same. Oral, anal, or verbal, is all sex to me.

La'shaun: Anyway, Malaya, back to your original question about "phone" sex.

Malaya: Like I was saying. I think the last time I tried talking "dirty," I may have said the wrong thing. That or I just was not seductive enough in my approach.

Essence: What did you say?

Malaya: I don't want to get into the semantics of it all.

Essence: La'shaun. She probably said something like, "I have to relieve myself, but when I get back, it's on."

La'shaun: Cut it out, Essence, before she hangs up again.

(Essence and La'shaun share laughs.)

La'shaun: Okay, let's change the subject. Essence, whatever happened with you and Tremaine?

Essence: That was just my bedroom buddy. I got bored with him. I told him our "arrangement" was no longer beneficial for me. I told him that it was not him rather it was me.

La'shaun: You didn't hit him with that old Mack daddy line?

Essence: It got a little ugly too.

Malaya: Did he abuse you verbally or physically?

Essence: Surely he cursed me and left. I will tell you'll this much, I am no longer dealing with a man that can't meet me where I am at sexually. If I do oral favors, the favor has to be mutual.

La'shaun: What if the sexual exchange is the greatest you have ever had?

Essence: It's no secret what sexual act every man wants. If he is not complaining to you, it's probably because he is getting the "job" done one way or the other. So I try to oblige as much as I can. Then they go and add rules. Bad enough sisters just started openly talking about fellatio in the '90s because for some reason brothers thought it was cool to tell all their friends if you performed such an act on them. Now they don't just want the act. Now you have to damn near turn your mouth into elastic or you'll hear, "Don't scrape." "Take the whole thing." "What about my scrotum?" Or "Okay, if you don't want to suck, can you at least kiss it one time." Heaven forbid I mention the swallowing issue. You are not always guaranteed its semen you're getting. All you get is a weak apology, and reassurance it won't happen the next time. So is it really too much of me to ask for my needs to be filled? Whatever happened to doing onto others as you want done onto you?

La'shaun: What about the guy that will take you out and thinks he bought the rights to your snack box?

Essence: I am not trying to get something for nothing here; favor for a favor.

La'shaun: What about when they mess your hair up after everything is all said and done?

Essence: My point again. If men want us to be all that we can be in that bedroom, they have got to give up some perks. I'm officially on strike like sweatshop workers across the country looking for better wages and treatment.

La'shaun: Men!

Essence: Their job is nowhere near as complex as ours. All they have to do is lick and rotate.

La'shaun: Some of them can't even do that right.

Essence: We have to lick, rotate, stretch, bend...It's like going to oral boot camp. Couldn't you hear them having a field day like, "Drop to your knees and give me ten solider."

La'shaun: Lay! Stop acting all innocent!

Malaya: I don't have wild sex stories. I just have sexual experiences that took the wrong turn.

Essence: Do tell.

Malaya: I was dealing with this really nice guy. The thing was, he didn't know how to use his tool. I never knew how to tell him because he was so nice.

La'shaun: So how did things end?

Malaya: This one time I could not stomach it any longer. Did either of you ever deal with a guy that had a very small penis, but a very big personality?

Antoinette Nyiann Lawson

Essence: Never me.

La'shaun: Umm, that would have to be, no for me too.

Malaya: At first, I wasn't as mad. I said to myself that it was not the size of the boat, but the motion in the ocean.

Essence: Sounds like you would have needed a monsoon.

Malaya: I mean this guy had a personality of a well-endowed man. I'm talking about this guy would try to put me in positions he knew he couldn't reach.

La'shaun: I guess he was trying to prove a point to himself. Who wants to come to the realization that they have short arms with deep pockets?

Malaya: I tried to work with him. I would only do missionary style. I tell you all no lies when I tell you his penis slipped out.

Essence: Say it isn't so.

Malaya: That was my breaking point.

La'shaun: That sounds like the same guy you said was cheap and something happened over a meal.

Essence: What guy? What meal?

Malaya: He wanted to order pizza, but before he ordered, he asked me if I wanted to go half on it. No sooner did I say no, the phone hung up. It wasn't like he was ordering from some well-established pizza shop. The worst part of it all was I had my girlfriend come up for the weekend. Prior to her coming up, I boasted about how smart and fine he was. Keshena laughs at me to this day about that.

Essence: What Keshena? Keshena with the big forehead?

Malaya: Yeah.

Essence: I didn't know the two of you still kept in touch? Anyway. La'shaun, how is your new hobby going?

La'shaun: What new hobby?

Essence: Stalking.

Malaya: You know you need to leave that man alone. For whatever reason he left, that's not relevant. If he was cheating, better that you found out when you did.

La'shaun: I know. I don't mean to go by his house. I just need to know if he really left me because he needed space or if it was someone else.

Essence: What difference does it make?

Malaya: How did you get his address anyway?

Essence: People cheat, for the most part because as the relationship gets old, you start to do things routinely. The things you use to do when you both first met goes out the window. I am not trying to rehash old feelings, but that's what happens.

Malaya: I was waiting for E to ask, but seems like she is waiting on you to come out with it. What caused the break between you and Lamont?

La'shaun: I notice he was acting a little strange at first. I was going to confront him about it, but I decided that I would rather keep it to myself. I figured, what good was it going to do anyway? I'd ask him, and he'll say no. I'll still walk away with a level of

disbelief. Or what if he said yeah, and I still
stayed with him?

Malaya: Love allows you to let certain things
move out of existence.

La'shaun: I loved him enough to at least
weigh out all my options first. Later on that
night, I prepared a candlelit dinner for the
two of us. The table was set for two, but
only one plate was filled. No sooner than
I finished cleaning and putting away the
dinner dishes, in strolls Lamont. I asked if
he had gotten the messages I sent to him
on his two-way. He said, "Baby, sit down,
we need to talk." Suddenly I felt compelled
to leave so he could not tell me what it was
he had to tell me. Before I could make it to
the loveseat, my tears beat me there. He
proceeded by telling me that yes he did get
the messages and he purposefully avoided
all my messages and me as well for the
past four weeks. He told me that he knew it
was immature and he should have told me
sooner, but at this point, the matter is not
a matter anymore. He went on to state that
we have talked about the same issue again
and again. He said that our relationship
had expired sexually. He brought up how he
would tell me to let him try it a certain way
or how he would tell me to let him put it
there. He said that everything with me was

predictable. He said, "When I turn you over, you turn yourself back over. I try to put it in other places; you tell me that's an exit only. I tell you to take deep breaths, you tell me its not ladylike to be on your knees." He went to say that he still loved me to the depths of his soul, it just so happened he loved himself a tad more. In which case, he had to do what was in his best interest. He said that I wasn't even open to watch adult videos. I asked why would he want me to do all these new things if I had already mastered my craft. He said that too much of anything is counterproductive. He said that if he gave me macaroni every single night, would I appreciate it just as I did the night before, and the night before last. He said that every time he tries to work with me, I am working against him. He went on to say rather than me trying something new, I set myself on doing things the way I'm use to doing them. Finally, he said that he was not going to beat a dead horse. Additionally, it always ends this way because he loves everything else about me. Usually, he'll try to sleep it off, and try to avoid me for as long as possible, thinking waiting would give him something to miss. But when he awakes, or saw me again, the same problems were there. Continuingly he said, truly, it's not just the sex. I will not lie and say it is not an important factor, but not the sole factor. It's gotten to the point were it's spiraled into a host of things. It's gotten to the point were it's down to the things you eat, the way you eat what you eat. The clothes you wear and how you wear them. He said that if we argue, he knew I would be the first to give in, despite if I still felt I were right. Most of the time, he said that I was right. It was past me just being predictable. It was me living for him and not for me. He didn't want me to think he was leaving because he wanted to. Rather, he was leaving because he had to. As a matter of fact, he said that he would not even want me to change because I would be doing it yet again for him and not for myself. He said that he would be back for his belongings at a better point in time. He said that he'd place his key to the apartment next to my heart so I would never forget him.

Essence: I bet you wanted to tell him that he would be back because she would never sex him the way you did. Hey wait, I tend to forget if that would have been a good thing or a bad thing.

Malaya: Essence. That's enough!

Essence: How do you lose your man, not someone you were kicking it with? Rather you lose your man because you won't change your sexual regime. All she had to do was slop the knob one good time and problem resolved and solved, all in one shot.

Malaya: You are missing the point, Essence! It's about La'shaun needing to find herself.

La'shaun: Now I guess it's back to the drawing board of meeting about five to ten guys a week. Getting acquainted and then deciding which one will be the one you sleep with and which one will be your get out of jail free card. I'm sure I am not the only one that has been broke and hungry before all at the same time. You call the guy that will do just about anything to see you. The only problem with that is you can't just eat and run (not if you want another free meal out of the deal); you have to put in time. Time being defined as going to the movies before dinner and listening to him tell you all about his life from age five. All while he diarrhea's from the mouth, you pretend to be attentive, because while he is telling you about his career, past relationships, friends, and family, the only thing you can think about is the guy that broke your heart. And how you wish it were him sitting across from you at the dinner table telling you about his goals and admirations. Now the night is coming to a close, along with your date. As he pulls up to your house, you watch him trying to find ways to proceed with extending the night. You could end the night by kissing him, but then you don't want to kiss everybody. Usually, you settle for the little kiss on the cheek and make your moves to head to your home. Upon getting in, you call up your girls and talk about whether or not you will date him again. Now remember, there are still the rest to weed out. Your process of elimination could start over the phone as well. This way you don't even have to waste your time going on an unnecessary date.

Essence: That's it?

La'shaun: What?

Essence: A dinner and a movie. If all he is offering you is a dinner and a movie, you should not have to contemplate another date.

Malaya: I have to agree with "E" on this one. Perhaps dating is not what you need right now. Take some time and work on yourself.

Essence: Get some toys while you're at it and work on your sex game too. I don't want you ever telling me again that your man left you because your freakiest position is missionary style. I have some tapes, magazines and/or tips I can give you.

Malaya: While, we will let you go. I'm sure you have some unfinished crying to get back to.

Essence: Don't let us keep you. However, I was serious about giving you those tapes and things.

Malaya: Hang up, Essence. Call me tomorrow, La'shaun, if you need anything.

The Rules of the Game

Essence: In order to keep your man, not only do you have to be willing to let yourself go; you have to be willing to see how far your man will let you go.

La'shaun: What do you mean?

Essence: Listen, rookie. It's no secret that a man's g-spot is around his anal area. So given the right moment, "boldly go where no man has hopefully not gone before."

La'shaun: Oh, to see if he is gay or not, right?

Essence: No, rookie, to see his reaction. Didn't you hear me just tell you his g-spot was there? It's just unfortunate we buy into the misbelieves handed down by "the powers that be" that if a man enjoys stimulation from his rectal area, he is some devilish deviant who has deviated from society's norms and shall burn in hell with the rest of us sinners who have pre-marital sex, and everything else that goes against the grain.

La'shaun: To be honest that's why I broke things off with Candy Bar.

Malaya: Who the hell is Candy Bar?

Essence: The guy she was dating before Lamont.

Malaya: Oh, right! I thought she told us that she broke things off with him because he was an exotic dancer?

Essence: Me too. Well, that's a rookie for you. Hello. She was dealing with someone by the name of Candy Bar. You would think that was the reason she stopped dealing with him!

Malaya: Well, I don't care what you say, E. I am not going anywhere near Malik's rear. You won't have me waking up to "It's Raining Men".

Essence: Okay, have it your way, I just want to leave you all with this. If what I say is false, tell me why do I have guys calling me more than the bill collectors? Why do you think that knucklehead was at my window in the wee hours of the morning singing "I Will Always Love You," by Whitney Houston and Dolly Parton?

Malaya: I do tip my hat off to you, La'shaun.

La'shaun: Why?

Malaya: Despite all the ups and downs you have had with black men, you still have not ventured to other avenues.

Essence: Not me. If you call getting laid and played a good thing, then yeah, I tip my hat off to her too. Consequently, when I do it, it serves another purpose.

La'shaun: Essence, how long did your last relationship last again?

Essence: Long enough for me to have enough money to start my own business. I'm not trying to say my relationships are long-lasted nor have the potential for longevity. I am saying that you could rest assured that any guy I have ever dealt with always brought something to the plate.

La'shaun: Well, I have my own money.

Essence: I as well. The issue is never about what I can do for myself. If that were the case, I would be by myself. The problem with your type is you'll want to claim independence and misuse the word. There is a difference between asking for something and being offered something. You have some men that won't ever offer. A woman of my caliber never has to ask for anything because my independence is clearly stated from the beginning. You are, however, the type of woman that does not get offered anything no way, so you tell yourself you don't need his money.

La'shuan: Well, I have my own money.

Essence: You're missing the point. Regardless if you accept or decline, the offer should always be extended to you.

Malaya: Damn, you might as well put your love vessel on the Internet for the highest bidder.

Essence: The problem here is the willingness or lack thereof to the acceptance of reality. I'm addressing this one to the both of you. If two adults consent to make bodily contact with one another, they also have to consent to the consequences that come along with it. Unfortunately, it is usually the woman left with dealing with her feelings after she and her partner has crossed sexual barriers. If a woman and a man cross-sexual lines, who is left with the possibility of spawning an embryo?

La'shuan: Both of them are.

Essence: Both parties are, but who will carry that baby for nine months? If the decision is to abort, whose body goes through the physical strain and emotional pain thereafter? If a man decides he wants to up and leave, who usually gets the short end of the stick? As soon as a woman decides to stand up for herself, she is underhanded and is only looking for a financial cushion. The two of you can accept or reject my opinion because in the end, that's all it is. As for myself, too many responsibilities come along once sexual barriers are crossed. As a result, I will always be ensured that any guy dealing with me has "something" to offer me.

La'shaun: You are always the first one to inform everyone that you are the liberating voice of relationships, but where is your man?Did you ever stop to think that you yourself misuse the word independence?

Essence: In what way do I do this?

La'shaun: I just feel that you are so caught up in being independent, you forget how to depend on anyone. A man needs to feel like you are dependent on him for something. If he feels that you are so independent, then why would you need him? A man needs to feel like a man and a woman needs to let him feel that way. Otherwise, you might as well be by your damn self.

Essence: Ironically, all this comes from a woman who is by herself. I'm giving you advice to assist you. I am alone by choice. You. Well, you are alone because of someone else's choice. While you are oversexed and underpaid, I'll be undersexed and overpaid. Keep letting those men use your body up like yesterday's news.

La'shaun: I am hanging up. I have some things to attend to.

Malaya: I think I burnt my cookies messing around with the two of you. I'm hanging up too.

Essence: No matter what the two of you say, something from nothing leads to nothing. But don't let me keep you ladies.

The End

When I was a little girl, I always believed
that the hardest thing I would have to face
throughout life is the loss of a loved one. In
growing, I believe what I've come to find to
be the hardest thing in life is being capable
of loving without anyone to give love to.
Being in love with someone who is not
capable or willing to love you back is a life
sentence of loneliness until you are able to
define what "true" love is.

Because I believe "true" love is something
that can only be found once you distinguish
"false" love from "true" love. Our "first"
love is usually our "false" love which
predetermines how we love, ultimately
causing us to be subjected to a host of bad
relationships because we are not yet able to
define what "true" love is. After we find what
"true" love is, we find "true" happiness.
Until we find this, we will continue to have
misguided relationships.

Someone once told me that "a man will be a man," and that it made no difference to her whether or not he engaged in questionable behaviors while he was out with the "boys" on his time, just as long as her time was her time. She also stated that she knew whom he was coming home to, so she felt secure with his false allegiance.

When we accept false allegiance, we unconsciously create a cycle. Unable to be with the one you love, you figure it's better to be with the one who loves you. As the pressure mounts, you selfishly stretch his love, trying to make it enough for you and him. Substituting your love with his love all while the one you love gives his love unconditionally to the one he loves. The sad part of it all is you want to love your new love, but you don't know how to not love your old love. So rather then being alone, you decide to take anybody's love and still be alone.

As women, we have to value or fertility and womanhood; this is fatal in our existence. We create a cycle where we encourage sexual involvements without any significant attachments. We date but do not exceed any expectations towards wedding vows. We look at the short-term picture but not the long-term picture. It's as if we are looking but not watching. Cycles of the way you date pour over to the way you live your life as a whole.

As you settle in your relationships, you settle in your career decisions and so on. A woman who is driven in her career is equally driven in her relationship because she has goals. As you settle for one thing, you began a domino effect, creating everything around you to slowly ascend.

On your trip to finding "true" love, don't make the mistake of looking outward and taking what society has defined as love. Ask yourself, "What makes me love me?" When you find that answer, you find yourself and you find "true" love.

ABOUT THE AUTHOR

I am a 25-year-old Bronx Native currently residing in Upstate, New York. I graduated from the University at Albany in Albany, New York in 2001 with my Bachelors of Arts in Sociology. I than went on to pursue my career in the Human Service fields. Throughout my career, I have dealt with persons that suffered from homelessness, mental illness, and substance abuse. Despite the obvious stressors, believe it or not, they all dealt with a broken heart.

Some have actually attributed their situations based on relationships that had gone bad; hence, equaling a broken heart. This book was designed to be an acting agent of foreshadows. I figured if one could see what was to come before it came, they could take preventive measures to prevent the trauma of heartache. Writing from a woman's perspective, I wanted to help women embrace their womanhood and finally be able to put themselves first.

For so long we see the "super woman" that works, cooks, cleans, and tends to the children. She tends to get so focused on doing things to appease everyone else, that she forgets to do basic things for herself. Slowly but surely she tends to slip into a stage of depression without even realizing it. What's worst than a woman who feels like she has but aside her goals, hopes and dreams to make her family a stronger unit? Hence, she comes home one day, and realizes that house is no longer a home.

What I wanted to draw out of this book is a sense of empowerment and remembrance of the "Women's Movement". Sometimes as women we get so caught with a man that we forget what it means to be a woman. We forget that a healthy relationship consist of two persons trying to come to some type of medium. Not one person trying to come to some type of medium. When everything is said and done, and the last page of this book is read, I want women to walk away with a sense of empowerment and remembrance of what it is to be a woman.

www.ingramcontent.com/pod-product-compliance
Lightning Source LLC
Chambersburg PA
CBHW030401290526
45785CB00004B/1849